Broadcasting

London: H M S O

Researched and written by Reference Services, Central Office of Information.

ISBN 0 11 701761 2

HMSO publications are available from:

HMSO Publications Centre
(Mail, fax and telephone orders only)
PO Box 276, London SW8 5DT
Telephone orders 071-873 9090
General enquiries 071-873 0011
(queuing system in operation for both numbers)
Fax orders 071-873 8200

HMSO Bookshops
49 High Holborn, London WC1V 6HB   071-873 0011
Fax 071-873 8200 (counter service only)
258 Broad Street, Birmingham B1 2HE   021-643 3740   Fax 021-643 6510
Southey House, 33 Wine Street, Bristol BS1 2BQ
0272 264306   Fax 0272 294515
9-21 Princess Street, Manchester M60 8AS   061-834 7201   Fax 061-833 0634
16 Arthur Street, Belfast BT1 4GD   0232 238451   Fax 0232 235401
71 Lothian Road, Edinburgh EH3 9AZ   031-228 4181   Fax 031-229 2734

HMSO's Accredited Agents
(see Yellow Pages)
and through good booksellers

Acknowledgments

This book has been compiled with the co-operation of several organisations. The Central Office of Information would like to thank all those who have contributed their comments, and in particular the Department of National Heritage, the BBC, the Independent Television Commission, the Radio Authority and the ITV Network Centre.

Contents

Introduction

Broadcasting in Britain[1] has traditionally been based on the principle that it is a public service accountable to the people through Parliament. While retaining the essential public service element, it now also embraces the principles of competition and choice.

This book outlines the Government's policies on broadcasting and looks at the broadcasting system in the light of changes resulting from the Broadcasting Act 1990. It describes the constitution and organisation of the BBC, the Independent Television Commission and the Radio Authority, and the services they provide. It gives brief accounts of the coverage of current affairs and politics and educational broadcasting, and refers to the contribution made by the broadcasting authorities to supporting the arts. It also touches upon the control of advertising, audience research and international relations, and summarises some recent technical developments.

[1] 'Britain' is used informally in this book to mean the United Kingdom of Great Britain and Northern Ireland; Great Britain comprises England, Scotland and Wales.

Structure of Broadcasting

Three public bodies have the main responsibility for television and radio services, to which nearly everyone has access throughout Britain:

—the British Broadcasting Corporation (BBC) broadcasts television and radio programmes;

—the Independent Television Commission (ITC) licenses and regulates non-BBC television services, including cable and satellite services; and

—the Radio Authority licenses and regulates all non-BBC radio services including cable and satellite services.

These authorities work to broad requirements and objectives defined by Parliament, but are otherwise independent in their day-to-day conduct of business.

The government department responsible for overseeing the broadcasting system is the Department of National Heritage, which was set up in April 1992, taking over the broadcasting responsibilities previously exercised by the Home Office. The Secretary of State for National Heritage is answerable to Parliament on broad policy questions.

During the last few years broadcasting in Britain has seen radical changes. The availability of more radio frequencies together with satellite, cable and microwave transmissions has made a greater number of local, national and international services possible. Moreover, the technical quality of sound and pictures is improving. In response to rapidly developing technology and rising public demand for a wide choice of programmes and services, the Government introduced the Broadcasting Act 1990 with the aim of making the regulatory framework for broadcasting more flexible and efficient and giving viewers and listeners access to a wider range of services. At the same time it aims to promote increased competition and maintain high standards of taste and decency. The Act takes full account of the need for programme quality and diversity, regional links, widespread ownership of broadcasting companies and proper geographical coverage, and makes provision for 'sharply focused statutory safeguards' backed by enforcement sanctions, including financial penalties.

Structure of Broadcasting

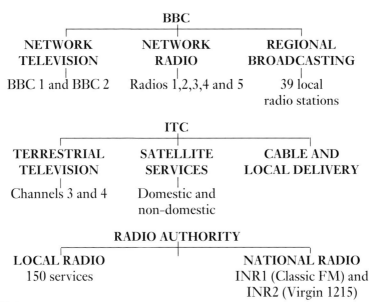

BBC

NETWORK TELEVISION	NETWORK RADIO	REGIONAL BROADCASTING
BBC 1 and BBC 2	Radios 1,2,3,4 and 5	39 local radio stations

ITC

TERRESTRIAL TELEVISION	SATELLITE SERVICES	CABLE AND LOCAL DELIVERY
Channels 3 and 4	Domestic and non-domestic	

RADIO AUTHORITY

LOCAL RADIO	NATIONAL RADIO
150 services	INR1 (Classic FM) and INR2 (Virgin 1215)

Note
INR = Independent National Radio Service

Television

Television viewing is by far Britain's most popular leisure pastime; about 93 per cent of households have a colour television set and almost two-thirds a video cassette recorder (VCR). On a typical day 80 per cent of the population tune into TV and 94 per cent watch at some time during the week. People spend an average of nearly four hours a day watching television including VCR playbacks. The most popular programmes attract audiences of over 16 million (see p. 5).

At present there are four terrestrial television channels offering a mixture of drama, light entertainment, films, sport, children's and religious programmes, news and current affairs, documentaries and educational programmes. The BBC provides two complementary national networks—BBC 1 and BBC 2—which are financed almost exclusively by licence fees. The ITC regulates two television services: ITV (Channel 3) and Channel 4. (In Wales S4C—Sianel Pedwar Cymru—broadcasts programmes on the Welsh fourth channel.) ITV and Channel 4 are expected to complement each other and are funded largely by advertising. All four channels broadcast on 625 lines UHF (ultra high frequency). Over 99 per cent of the population lives within range of transmission.

In recent years the allocation of viewing between the BBC, ITV and Channel 4 has been at a fairly constant ratio. More recently cable and satellite have accounted for almost 5 per cent of total viewing, and around 30 per cent in homes receiving these services.

British television programmes continue to win many international awards, and Britain is one of the world's leading exporters of television productions. In 1991 British television companies received £132 million in export earnings and there are few countries where British programmes have not been shown.

Table 1: TV Ratings for 17–23 May 1993

BBC1	Millions	BBC2	Millions	ITV	Millions	C4	Millions
1 EastEnders (Tue/Sun)	15.47	Have I Got News For You	6.82	Coronation Street (Mon)	17.38	Brookside (Mon/Sat)	6.43
2 Neighbours (Mon)	14.94	Delia Smith's Summer Collection	3.76	Heartbeat	13.17	Roseanne	4.29
3 Match of the Day	13.44	The Fresh Prince of Bel-Air	3.48	Peak Practice	12.79	Grow Your Greens	3.69
4 Birds of a Feather	9.47	Gardeners' World	3.44	Home and Away (Mon)	12.32	Clive Anderson Talks Back	3.57
5 999	9.08	Quantum Leap	3.38	The Bill (Tue)	11.71	The Crystal Maze	3.37
6 On the Up	8.14	Savage Island	3.17	Taggart	10.89	Eat Your Greens	3.35
7 A Question of Guilt	7.98	Top Gear	3.14	Short Circuit II	10.69	Fifteen to One (Thu)	3.32
8 Spacecamp	7.27	Night Shift	3.06	Emmerdale (Tue)	9.64	The Golden Palace	3.22
9 Nine O'Clock News (Thu)	7.23	Sunday Grandstand	2.81	Someone to Watch Over Me	9.51	Cheers	3.21
10 An Officer and a Gentleman	6.74	Bad Company	2.77	Busman's Holiday (Joint 9th)	9.51	Surgical Spirit	2.99

Source: BARB (see p. 71)

Radio

Practically every home has a radio set, and the widespread owner-ship of portable sets and car radios means that people can listen to radio throughout the day. Almost half the population listen to the radio on a normal day and 76 per cent do so over the week. Average listening time is around an hour and a half a day. Around a third will listen to the BBC on any given day and 58 per cent do so in the course of a week. Fifty-three per cent of the population now listens to some form of commercial radio each week.

The BBC has five national networks, which transmit all types of music, news, current affairs, drama, education, sport and a range of features programmes. The first national commercial radio station, Classic FM, began broadcasting in September 1992; the second—Virgin 1215—started in April 1993. A third national independent station, which must be mainly speech-based, is planned.

There are 39 BBC local radio stations serving England and the Channel Islands, and regional and community radio services in Scotland, Wales and Northern Ireland. Some 150 independent local radio (ILR) services are also available to local communities throughout Britain. Further local stations are planned. About 90 per cent of the population is within range of BBC or ILR stations. The stations supply a comprehensive service of local news and information, sport, music and other entertainment, education, consumer advice and coverage of local events. Phone-in programmes allowing listeners to express their views on air are popular.

Wavebands

Britain's domestic services are broadcast across three wavebands, FM (or VHF), Medium Wave (sometimes referred to as AM), and Long Wave (although BBC Radio 4 is the only British service using it).

European services can to some extent be received over most of the country but not on FM. Nearly all radio sets offer FM and MW, with most covering all three bands. However, more and more services, both on BBC and in the independent sector, are broadcast on one frequency only rather than 'simulcast' on FM and MW in line with government policy.

Broadcasting Act 1990

The Government's proposals for reforming broadcasting, now incorporated in the Broadcasting Act 1990, were set out in the White Paper *Broadcasting in the '90s: Competition, Choice and Quality*, published in 1988. These proposals were informed by the findings and recommendations of three official reports: the Peacock report on broadcasting (1986); a Green Paper on radio (1987); and the main report of the House of Commons Home Affairs Committee inquiry into broadcasting (1988). For details of all the above, see Further Reading, p. 84.

Guiding Principles

The guiding principles behind the Broadcasting Act 1990 are listed below.

—Broadcasting services must remain independent of Government editorially and, as far as possible, in economic and regulatory terms.

—Because of broadcasting's power, immediacy and influence, there remains the need for regulation to guarantee standards, particularly regarding taste and decency and to protect viewers and listeners against exploitation and poor quality programming.

—The differences between radio and television as broadcasting media call for different control arrangements.

—New services, programmes and methods of transmission and payment should not be artificially restricted. Direct payment for television through subscription should be encouraged and advertising and sponsorship rules should be more flexible.

—Restrictive practices should be discouraged and it must be made as easy as possible for new services to be launched.

—There should be a greater separation between the various functions which make up broadcasting and which have previously been carried out by one organisation. These include programme production, assembly of individual programmes into channels ('channel packaging') and transmission. Independent producers should be given more scope.

—Broadcasting companies and organisations should be run efficiently to enable them to offer audiences good value for money and compete effectively with one another and with overseas broadcasters.

—Through greater competition, pressures should be exerted to hold down television advertising rates.

Changes Introduced by the Act

The Broadcasting Act 1990 overhauled the regulation of independent television and radio and allowed the introduction of additional services.

In January 1991 the Independent Broadcasting Authority (IBA) was replaced by the Independent Television Commission (ITC), the Radio Authority, and a new transmission and engineering company (National Transcommunications Limited—see p. 9). At the same time the Cable Authority, set up in 1984, was made part of the ITC and the Radio Authority. The ITC does not have the former IBA's detailed involvement in scheduling but has wider powers than the IBA to enforce licence conditions and ownership rules.

Both the ITC and the Radio Authority issue licences to commercial broadcasters and enforce rules to ensure diversity of ownership. The organisations were initially able to take out government loans, but are obliged to repay these and to support themselves from licence fees at the earliest possible date. Although regulation is light, rules are enforced so that ownership remains widely spread and undue concentrations and cross-media ownership are kept in check.

Provision was made in the Broadcasting Act for the former IBA's television and radio transmission networks to be privatised. In 1991 the IBA's networks and other facilities were transferred to a new public company—National Transcommunications Limited (NTL). NTL was then sold for £70 million to a new company formed for the purpose by Mercury Asset Management. NTL, which is now wholly privately owned, transmits television services for the independent television companies, Channel 4, S4C, and radio services for about 50 independent local radio stations. It also has a research and development capability. The company operates from over 950 transmitting sites and employs about 750 people.

Recognising the importance of public service broadcasting, the 1990 Act made no change to the BBC's cornerstone public service role of providing high quality programming throughout the full range of public tastes and interests; the essential programming remits of all BBC domestic services remain unchanged.

The Organisation of Broadcasting Authorities

The BBC

The constitution, finances and obligations of the BBC are governed by a Royal Charter, which expires in December 1996, and by a Licence and Agreement. Those of the ITC and the Radio Authority are governed by the Broadcasting Act 1990.

Administration

The BBC, which was set up in 1927, has a board of 12 governors, including the chairman, vice-chairman and a national governor each for Scotland, Wales and Northern Ireland. The board is appointed by the Queen in Council on the advice of the Government and is ultimately responsible for all aspects of broadcasting on the BBC. The governors appoint the Director-General, the Corporation's chief executive officer, who heads the board of management, the body in charge of the daily running of the services.

The BBC has a strong regional structure. The three English regions—BBC North, BBC Midlands & East and BBC South—and the Scottish, Welsh and Northern Ireland national regions, make programmes for their local audiences as well as contributing to the national network (see p. 26).

The National Broadcasting Councils for Scotland, Wales and

Northern Ireland provide advice on the policy and content of television and radio programmes intended mainly for reception in their areas. Local radio councils, representative of the local community, advise on the development and operation of the BBC's local radio stations.

Finance

The domestic services of the BBC are financed almost wholly from the sale of television licences. Households with television must buy an annual licence costing (from April 1993) £83 for colour and £27.50 for black and white. Over 19.6 million licences were current in April 1992, of which about 18.4 million were for colour. More than two-thirds of expenditure on domestic services relates to television.

Table 2: How the Licence Income was Spent in 1991–92

	£million
BBC 1	593.7
BBC 2	306.2
Radio networks	238.7
Regional broadcasting	226.5
Licence fee collection	92.5
Restructuring costs	70.5
Re-equipment	43.3
Net other income	(16.9)
Deficit	(68.4)
Total	**1,486.1**

Licence Fees

In 1991 the BBC took over from the Home Office responsibility for administering the licence fee system. TVL, a subsidiary company of the Post Office, undertakes the licence administration on behalf of the BBC. Since 1988 annual rises in the licence fee have been linked to the rate of inflation; this is intended to further improve the BBC's efficiency and encourage it to continue developing alternative sources of revenue. A review to assess progress will be made before 1994. The longer-term future funding of the BBC will be considered as part of the Charter review (see p. 13).

Licence income is supplemented by profits from trading activities, such as television programme exports, sale of recordings and publications connected with BBC programmes, hire and sale of educational films, film library sales, and exhibitions based on programmes. The BBC meets the cost of its local radio stations. BBC World Service Radio is financed by a grant-in-aid from the Foreign & Commonwealth Office (£163 million in 1992–93), while BBC World Service Television (see p. 29) is self-funding.

Producer Choice

In April 1993 the BBC introduced Producer Choice, a new resource management system requiring those of its departments responsible for providing production facilities and services to compete with outside contractors. The system aims to provide value for money by giving greater freedom to programme makers, enabling them to choose the best and most competitively priced production resources available.

Future of the BBC

A government discussion paper, *The Future of the BBC: A Consultation Document* (see Further Reading), setting out the framework for a debate on the future of the BBC, was published in November 1992. The paper stresses the need for a wide-ranging debate, covering all aspects of the BBC's work and structure.

The paper states that the range and quality of the BBC's radio and television programmes, and its technical excellence, have received worldwide recognition. It notes, however, that broadcasting has changed rapidly since the present Charter was granted in 1981 and believes it may be necessary to consider radical changes in the way the BBC operates. The Government believes the BBC should continue as a major broadcasting organisation, with special responsibilities for public service broadcasting, but it considers that the BBC cannot continue as if nothing had changed since 1981.

Future Aims of Public Service Broadcasting

The paper asks if all public service broadcasting should become the responsibility of a new Public Service Broadcasting Council, which could promote, regulate and fund public service broadcasting on all channels, including those provided by the BBC. While this Council would ensure diversity in the range of programmes, 'such a Council would hold the purse-strings to sizeable resources and it would clearly be unacceptable if this power led to the imposition of a single cultural or editorial viewpoint'.

Nature of Programmes and Services

At present the BBC is expected to broadcast programmes of information, entertainment and education. The paper asks if the BBC should continue to provide a wide range of programmes, or whether it should concentrate on the kind of programmes which are unlikely to be broadcast by other television channels or radio stations.

The paper says that 'if the BBC is to continue to be the main public service broadcaster in Britain, the objectives of public service broadcasting will have to be built into its future plans, programmes and finances'. There should be a coherent framework for the range of programmes and services which the BBC will be expected to provide, its organisation and method of funding, the extent of its other activities, and 'the arrangements for editorial decisions, and for public accountability both for programmes and value for money'.

On radio, '. . . further rationalisation may be necessary. Given the variety of other radio services, it is arguable that the BBC radio should no longer try to broadcast such a wide range of programmes, with the aim that everyone should find something of interest'.

Funding

The paper asks whether the television licence fee should continue to be the main source of the BBC's funds or whether its services should be paid for wholly or partly in other ways, such as advertising, sponsorship, taxation or subscription.

Although it describes the licence fee as 'an oddity', the paper concludes that 'so far no one has devised an obviously better system'. 'The licence fee is readily understood. It guarantees the BBC a regular income and it preserves the arm's-length relationship between the broadcasters and the Government.' Advertising, it says, would not provide sufficient funding and would jeopardise the financial stability of the ITV companies. Moreover, BBC programmes 'would have to attract sufficiently large, or affluent, audiences to persuade advertisers to pay enough to cover the programme costs'. This might put the BBC under pressure 'to increase its audiences at the expense of programmes of interest to smaller, or poorer audiences'. As for subscription, this 'discourages people from sampling a wide range of programmes and could reduce the availability of programmes for those less able to pay'.

Whatever the method of financing, 'the BBC needs to give value for money and to demonstrate that it is doing so. It needs to improve the efficiency of its activities each year, while maintaining the quality of its programmes'. According to the paper: 'efficiency can also be improved through greater use of market testing and contracting out, by employing contract staff, and by moving more BBC functions to areas where rents and costs are cheaper than in London'.

Accountability

Traditionally, governments have not intervened in decisions about programmes nor in the day-to-day management of the BBC. The paper says that the Government has no intention of changing that position. However, if the BBC is to continue as a public service broadcaster, there should be ways of ensuring that it is responsive to its audiences, accountable for the services it provides and that it is efficient and gives value for money. The paper asks if a better framework can be designed to achieve this without diluting the BBC's editorial independence. 'If the BBC is given a new remit for its services, then new measures for audience reaction are likely to be needed. These could look at the purpose of individual programmes, the likely audience and the degree of audience appreciation.'

Extending Choice

In November 1992 the BBC published *Extending Choice: The BBC's Role in the New Broadcasting Age*, its first contribution to the debate on the future of the organisation. The discussion document details four areas in which the BBC can make a special contribution in extending choice for viewers and listeners. According to the document, the BBC should offer:

—impartial, authoritative news and information across a range of television and radio channels to enable a properly informed debate on important issues;

—a showcase for traditional and contemporary British culture and fresh and innovative entertainment, reflecting Britain's rich cultural heritage and encouraging new talent and ideas in drama, comedy, entertainment, music, the arts, sport and children's programmes;

—programmes which help to educate and inform, like documentaries, science and natural history, religious broadcasting and services for schools, the Open University and adult education; and

—communication between Britain and overseas through World Service Radio, the fast-developing World Service television and international sales of BBC programmes.

The Independent Television Commission

The ITC, which replaced the IBA and the Cable Authority in January 1991, is responsible for licensing and regulating all non-BBC television services operating in or from Britain. These include:

—Channel 3 (ITV—see p. 34);

—Channel 4 (see p. 37);

—the proposed Channel 5 (see p. 39);

—cable and other local delivery services (see p. 43);

—independent teletext services (see p. 46); and

—domestic and non-domestic satellite services available to viewers in Britain (see p. 48).

The ITC has the duty to ensure:

—that a wide range of television programme services is available throughout Britain and that, taken as a whole, they are of a high quality and appeal to a variety of tastes and interests; and

—fair and effective competition in the provision of such services.

It awards major broadcasting licences by competitive tender to the highest bidders satisfying stipulated quality tests (see p. 36). It regulates its services through licence conditions and through codes on programme content, advertising, sponsorship and technical standards (see p. 64). It does not produce or make programmes itself.

Until December 1992, when the former ITV franchises ended (see p. 35), the ITC continued to fulfil IBA's obligations towards the ITV programme contracts, being legally responsible for broadcasting programmes shown on ITV, Channel 4 and direct broadcasting by satellite services (DBS). In January 1993, when the new Channel 3 licences came into effect, the ITC ceased to be responsible for broadcasting programmes; these responsibilities have now passed to the new licensees.

The ITC monitors the licences and licence conditions but is not involved in detailed scheduling of programmes. It has wider powers than the IBA to enforce licence conditions and rules

designed to limit cross-media ownership and excessive concentration of ownership. The major change is from a system which
includes prior restraint—pre-vetting of programmes and
schedules—to one of monitoring services regulated in the first
instance by the licensees themselves.

The ITC has ten members including a chairman and a deputy
chairman, all appointed by the Government. They are supported
by a range of specialist staff and by ten regional consultative councils (see below). The ITC is advised by committees on educational
broadcasting, religious broadcasting, charitable appeals and
advertising.

There are ten regional Viewer Consultative Councils: seven in
England and one for each of the national regions in Wales, Scotland
and Northern Ireland. The Councils comment on the commercial
services' programmes.

The Radio Authority

The Radio Authority, which took over responsibility for independent radio from the IBA in January 1991, licenses and regulates all
independent radio services in Britain. The Authority has three
main tasks:

—to plan frequencies;

—to appoint licensees with a view to widening listener choice; and

—to regulate programming and advertising.

The underlying principles of independent local radio (ILR)
are similar to those of ITV (see p. 34). The programme companies
operate under licence to the Radio Authority and are financed
mainly by advertising revenue. Licences for many existing operators will expire during 1994–96.

The Radio Authority awards national radio licences by competitive tender to the highest cash bidders. Local radio licences are not allocated by competitive tender; the success of licence applications is in part determined by audience demand, and the extent to which prospective stations would increase variety.

The Authority is required to publish codes to which licensees must adhere. These cover engineering, programmes, advertising and sponsorship. There are also rules on ownership (see below). Like the ITC, the Radio Authority carefully monitors the licences and licence conditions.

The Authority's sole source of income comes from the annual fees paid to it by licensees.

Ownership Rules for Independent Broadcasting

The Broadcasting Act 1990 established clearer and more extensive ownership rules. These are designed to enable the ITC and the Radio Authority to keep ownership of the broadcasting media widely spread and to prevent unhealthy concentrations and cross-media ownership. Under the rules:

—no organisation from outside the European Community (EC) is allowed to acquire a controlling interest in a domestic broadcasting licence (exceptions are local delivery franchises and satellite services not using British broadcasting frequencies);

—national newspapers are allowed a maximum 20 per cent stake in DBS channels, Channels 3 and 5, and national and local radio (see p. 21);

—public telecommunications operators are prevented from having a controlling interest in any Channel 3, Channel 5, national radio or domestic satellite licence;

—political bodies and local authorities are barred from holding any licences; and

—religious groups are allowed to compete for licences to have their own local radio stations. They can also seek licences for short duration, limited geographical area radio licences and for some cable and non-domestic satellite television channels.

Subject to certain qualifications (see below), the maximum number of licences which any one person may hold within a particular category of licence is:

—two in the case of regional Channel 3 services;

—one in the case of the national Channel 3 service;

—one in the case of Channel 5;

—one in the case of national radio services; and

—20 in the case of local radio services or the six largest local radio services, subject to a maximum of 15 per cent of the total points in a scheme based on population coverage.

There are also limits on overlapping areas.

Licences for Channels 3 and 5

Channel 3 regional licence areas have been classified by the Government as either large or small according to their share of total advertising revenue; at present there are nine large and five small licence areas. A company can hold two Channel 3 regional licences, but no single group or company can own two large licences. Nor can an applicant own a national and a regional Channel 3 licence. Bodies within the European Community but outside Britain may hold licences.

From the date of the award of Channel 3 licences up to the end of 1993, takeovers will require ITC approval. From 1994 onwards the ITC must be satisfied that any company taking over a licensee is suitable and able to meet all the conditions of the licence; otherwise the licence will be revoked.

Anyone owning two regional Channel 3 licences—or one licence in the case of national Channel 3 and Channel 5—is allowed to have a maximum 20 per cent stake in one additional such licence, and a maximum 5 per cent holding in any further licences. People without a controlling interest in any licence are allowed to have more than a 20 per cent interest in two regional or one national licence, a maximum 20 per cent stake in one further such licence and a maximum 5 per cent holding in any additional licences. (For details of the licences awarded by the ITC in October 1991, see p.35.)

Broadcasting Complaints Commission

The Broadcasting Complaints Commission, which was established in 1981, is an independent statutory complaints body, financed by money voted by Parliament. Appropriate contributions are recovered from the BBC, S4C, the ITC and the Radio Authority. It deals with complaints of unfair treatment in broadcast programmes and of unwarranted infringement of privacy in programmes or in their preparation. Its function extends to all sound, television and licensed cable and satellite programme services including advertisements and teletext transmission and programmes broadcast by the BBC's World Service.

Complaints of unjust or unfair treatment must be made by someone who took part in the programme or with a direct interest in the treatment complained of; complaints of unwarranted infringement of privacy must be made by the person whose privacy was infringed. Complaints might include that a broadcaster trespassed on private land to film programme material or that a person's words have been used out of context to distort his or her meaning.

The Commission may decide to hold a hearing to consider a complaint and can require its findings to be broadcast and published in writing. In 1991–92 it received 1,048 complaints. Of these, 120 were within the Commission's jurisdiction. It issued 54 adjudications, and a further 65 were under consideration at the end of the year. Details of complaints made and decisions reached are published annually.

BBC Television and Radio Services

BBC Television

Apart from a break during the second world war (1939–45), the BBC has been providing regular television broadcasts since 1936, when it began the first public high definition service in the world. The BBC transmits more than 17,000 hours of programmes a year for national and regional audiences. Its two channels— BBC 1 and BBC 2—reach 19.6 million licence-paying households throughout Britain.

As a public service broadcaster, the BBC is committed to reflecting the full range of opinion and cultures in Britain in its programme schedules. In a typical week, 94 per cent of the population watches television, with 93 per cent tuning into the BBC.

The two channels, BBC 1 and BBC 2, are scheduled in a complementary way to cater simultaneously for people of different interests. Although both services cover the whole range of television output, they differentiate as follows:

—BBC 1 presents a wide range of programmes, including news and current affairs, major documentaries, sport, popular drama and light entertainment, and children's programmes;

—BBC 2 presents music and the arts, new talent and ideas, innovative documentaries, sport, international films and serious drama, and is a forum for debate.

As well as the wide range of material for the general network audience, both BBC channels broadcast programmes for schools, Open University students and those interested in continuing education (see p. 55). BBC 1 takes up 40 per cent of the total BBC income and BBC 2 20 per cent.

Programmes for both networks are produced mainly in London and by the three network production centres at Birmingham, Bristol and Manchester. They are also produced by the national regional centres in Belfast, Glasgow and Cardiff, and increasingly, by independent producers who are commissioned in every area of programming, excluding news and news-related daily current affairs programmes, continuity and Open University output. Programmes for local audiences are also produced by the BBC's national regions and by the three English regions—BBC North, BBC Midlands & East and BBC South—from studios in their areas.

Under the Broadcasting Act 1990 both the BBC and commercial licensees (see p. 35) are required to commission at least 25 per cent of their original television programmes (except news-related output) from independent companies by 1993–94. In working towards this quota, the BBC's policy is to commission programmes from network and regional centres across the range of programming, from documentary to drama.

BBC Subscription Television Ltd

BBC Subscription Television Ltd is a commercially run subsidiary of the BBC created in 1990 to run subscription-financed television services in the night hours under the name BBC SELECT. Broadcasting is between 2.00 and 6.00 hours on BBC 1 and BBC 2, when the BBC is off the air. Programmes are designed to be video recorded and replayed at a time to suit individual viewers. They are transmitted in scrambled form and unscrambled by decoder connected to the subscriber's video cassette recorder. Initially BBC SELECT has been broadcasting professional, training and educational services tailored for lawyers, accountants, business executives and language learners. As these become established, consumer interest services are being added to cover home education, leisure and community interests.

Most services on BBC SELECT are provided by outside companies who finance their production mainly from subscription income but also from the advertising and sponsorship which will be permitted on these scrambled services. The Executive Business Club, a service providing management training to companies, was the first to be launched in July 1992, followed by services for accountants and lawyers.

As well as pay services, some programming is transmitted during the night freely available for anyone to watch like any other BBC programme. The first service, 'The Way Ahead', a series on disability allowances, produced by the Department of Social Security, was launched in January 1992. Other series are designed for nurse training and for company assistant general managers. These programmes cannot carry advertising or sponsorship.

BBC Network Radio

BBC Network Radio broadcasts each year around 35,000 hours of programmes on its five networks, which serve an audience of 27 million in Britain.

—Radio 1 broadcasts rock and pop music 24 hours a day.

—Radio 2 (on FM only) transmits popular music and light entertainment also for 24 hours a day.

—Radio 3 (also on FM only) broadcasts mainly classical music, but presents jazz, drama, poetry, short stories and talks as well. The network draws on the resources of the BBC's five symphony orchestras (see p. 60).

—Radio 4 is the main speech network, providing the principal news and current affairs service, together with series on medicine, science, religion, law, natural history, books, money, gardening and programmes for people with disabilities. These are supplemented by humour with sit-coms, quizzes and satire. The network also carries parliamentary coverage.

—Radio 5 (on medium wave only) is dedicated chiefly to sport, education and speech programmes for young people (see p. 56) and selections of programmes from the World Service. The network was created by a rationalisation of BBC radio services in preparation for the surrender of frequencies required by the Government for the commercial networks set up under the terms of the Broadcasting Act 1990.

BBC Regional Broadcasting

The three national regions—Scotland, Wales and Northern Ireland—and the three English regions—North, Midlands & East, and South—employ a quarter of the BBC staff and make a range of programmes for local, regional and national audiences. Around 4,000 hours of network radio and 2,000 hours of network television programmes come from its production centres outside London. In addition, BBC Scotland, Wales and Northern Ireland make many television programmes for their own audiences, and provide radio services on Radio Scotland, Radio Wales and Radio Cymru and Radio Ulster. Each has community or 'opt out' stations to serve the interests of local audiences.

The three English regions also provide their own television news, parliamentary and current affairs programmes covering the issues and concerns of local audiences.

BBC Local Radio

A total of 10 million listeners a week tune in to the BBC's 39 local radio stations in England. They broadcast news and information, and as well as reflecting important local issues, they play a key role in the BBC's national and international newsgathering operation.

BBC World Service

BBC World Service Radio

The BBC is an international broadcaster. It broadcasts its long-established World Service radio in English and 39 other languages. Output amounts to 820 weekly hours of language transmissions. BBC World Service radio has the largest audience of any international radio broadcaster—120 million regular listeners worldwide. It grew out of the Empire Service, which began in 1932. The main objectives of the Service are to give unbiased news, reflect British opinion, and project British life, culture and developments in science and industry. Unlike the BBC domestic television and radio services, the World Service is not financed by a licence fee on set owners, but by a grant from Parliament. In 1992–93 this amounted to £163 million. News bulletins, current affairs programmes, political commentaries and topical magazine programmes form the main part of the output. These are supplemented by a sports service, music, drama, and general entertainment.

The languages in which the World Service broadcasts and the number of hours devoted to each are prescribed by the Government. In June 1992 the World Service began broadcasting in Ukrainian, the first new language it had introduced for ten years. Otherwise the BBC has full responsibility and is completely independent in determining the content of news and other programmes.

There are broadcasts by radio for 24 hours a day in English, supplemented at peak listening times by programmes of special interest to Africa, East Asia, South Asia, Europe, the Caribbean and the Falkland Islands.

BBC World Service news bulletins and other programmes are re-broadcast by some 450 radio and cable stations in over 80 countries, which receive the programmes by satellite. Two World Service departments also specialise in supplying radio material for re-broadcast.

BBC Transcription and BBC Topical Tapes

BBC Transcription sells BBC radio programmes to overseas broadcasters in over 100 countries, while BBC Topical Tapes airmails some 250 tapes of original programmes to subscribers in 50 countries each week. Topical Tapes are available for educational use overseas and in Britain.

BBC English

BBC English is the most extensive language-teaching venture in the world. English lessons are broadcast daily by radio with explanations in some 30 languages, including English, and re-broadcast by many radio stations. BBC English television programmes are also shown in more than 90 countries. A range of printed, audio and video material accompanies these programmes.

BBC Monitoring

BBC Monitoring listens to and reports on foreign broadcasts, providing a daily flow of significant news and comment from overseas to the BBC and the Government. This information is also sold to the press, private sector companies, academic staff and public bodies. Jointly with its US partner, it monitors broadcasts from about 130 countries. Information and documentation from this joint operation is available in a 24-hour teleprinted newsfile and two publications, which can be bought by subscription.

BBC World Service Television

BBC World Service Television was set up in 1991 to establish a worldwide television service. The company is a wholly owned self-funding subsidiary of the BBC and receives no revenue from either the TV licence fees or the Government. BBC World Service Television aims to offer a global service by 1993, adopting funding formulas and combinations of programmes to suit each region. At present it provides services to three continents.

Europe

A subscription channel in Europe provides an 18-hours-a-day service (15 hours at weekends), based on a mixture of BBC 1 and BBC 2 programmes. It offers comedy, drama, light entertainment, sport, children's programmes, documentaries, news, and current affairs. There is also a 30-minute international bulletin from BBC World Service Television News, together with weather and business reports. Viewers receive the service by cable or direct to their homes, using special decoders.

Asia

A 24-hour news and information channel is available throughout Asia. Launched in November 1991, this is the BBC's first 24-hour international channel. The service is one of the channels offered throughout Asia by the commercial company STAR TV and is available as a terrestrial service in the Gulf on Bahrain TV. Programmes include hourly international news bulletins, followed by special bulletins of Asian news, weather and business reports, current affairs and other factual programmes from BBC television.

The BBC service on STAR TV is funded by advertising. The channel is compiled and scheduled by the BBC, which retains editorial control. It is transmitted by satellite from London to Hong Kong, where advertising is added by STAR TV before distribution throughout Asia. The service is available free to homes equipped with their own satellite dishes.

Africa

A news and information channel is shown throughout Africa. Launched in April 1992 in collaboration with the South African-based company M-Net, this broadcasts daily for 11 hours. Like the Asian service, programmes include international news, weather and business reports, and BBC current affairs and documentary series. The service is available to viewers with the appropriate satellite reception equipment and in countries where national broadcasters make the service part of their regular output.

BBC World Service Television, together with Nissho Iwai, a trading company based in Tokyo, plan to launch a 24-hour news and information channel in Japan in 1994.

BBC Commercial Services

BBC Enterprises Ltd

BBC Enterprises Ltd is the commercial arm of the BBC, a wholly owned subsidiary selling programmes and programme-related material throughout the world and reinvesting the profits in new productions. As well as selling programmes and promoting co-productions with other broadcasters, BBC Enterprises Ltd has developed its publishing activities, magazines, books and audio and video cassettes based on BBC programmes and archives or providing supporting material for viewers and listeners. These include educational and training material. A recent development has been BBC Subscription Television (see p. 24).

Turnover in 1991–92 was £180 million excluding £30 million in co-production finance also raised for BBC Television.

Library and Information Research Services

The BBC provides a wide range of background material through its network of libraries, archival collections, specialist services, international databases and cuttings libraries (with a stock of 24 million classified cuttings and a daily addition rate of some 2,000 new cuttings from the national and provincial press). The Research Libraries have a stock of some 200,000 books and substantial numbers of periodicals, maps and official publications. Access for non-BBC users is by individual enquiry or as a regular service on a commercial basis through the BBC Data Enquiry Service.

Specialist BBC Libraries

—The Radio Drama Script Information Unit holds 60,000 scripts, mostly on microfilm, dating from 1922. Mainly for internal use, these are also sent to radio stations throughout the world. The Unit is open to researchers by appointment only.

—The BBC Photograph Library has an archive collection of over 2 million BBC photographs dating from 1922. It provides access to archive and semi-current material to book and magazine publishers and other commercial clients.

—The Music Library has a collection of 3 million items, including scores, parts, books and periodicals covering the whole serious music repertoire. Its main objective is to supply music for broadcast performance.

—The Popular Music Library covers all aspects of music from the nineteenth century to the present. It holds manuscripts and printed orchestral arrangements of light and popular music, song copies and albums, vocal scores, piano and instrumental solos. Public access is by prior arrangement, and a musical hire scheme is in operation.

—The Sound Library contains 500,000 sound archive recordings and a changing stock of 90,000 current recordings containing 60,000 radio programmes or inserts for programme making. It also has some 20,000 recorded sound effects and an index of domestic radio programmes. Licensing of archive material for commercial and other non-BBC use is possible.

—The BBC Gramophone Library Catalogue contains over 2.5 million comprehensively detailed performance entries used to index the 1.2 million records on the library's shelves, and is considered to be the most complete record of commercial releases in Britain from 1888 to 1993. The catalogue is now available commercially on CD–ROM (compact disc–read only memory).

Independent Broadcasting

Independent Television

The first regular ITV (independent television) programmes began in London in 1955. Although there are very many programmes which are broadcast nationally, the first independent television channel was, from the beginning, a regional system. ITV programmes are broadcast 24 hours a day in all parts of the country. About one-third of output comprises informative programmes—news, documentaries, and programmes on current affairs, education and religion. The remainder cover sport, comedy, drama, game shows, films and a range of other programmes with popular appeal. Over half of the programmes are produced by the programme companies and ITN (see p. 37). Many programme companies sell their programmes overseas.

ITV (Channel 3) Programme Companies

The ITV system is referred to as Channel 3 in the Broadcasting Act 1990. ITV is made up of 15 regionally based independent television companies which are licensed by the ITC to supply programmes in the 14 independent television geographical regions. (Two companies share the contract for London, one providing programmes during weekdays and the other at the weekend.) An additional ITC licensee provides a national breakfast-time service, transmitted on the ITV network.

The licensees operate on a commercial basis, deriving most of their revenue from the sale of advertising time. The financial resources, advertising revenue and programme production of the companies vary considerably, depending largely on the size of population in the areas in which they operate. Although newspapers may acquire an interest in programme companies, there are safeguards to ensure against concentration of media ownership, thereby protecting the public interest (see p. 19).

Each programme company plans the content of the programmes to be broadcast in its area. These are produced by the company itself, or by other programme companies or bought from elsewhere.

Renewal of Licences

The ITV licences for the 15 regional companies and the single national breakfast-time licence, which came up for renewal at the end of 1992, were awarded by the ITC in October 1991. Twelve existing franchise holders were awarded licences (see Table 3).

In addition, four new companies were awarded licences:

—Meridian was awarded the franchise for south and south-east England, previously held by TVS Television Ltd, with a winning bid of £36,523,000;

—Carlton Television Ltd was awarded the franchise for the London weekday service, previously held by Thames Television plc (winning bid: £43,170,000);

—Westcountry Television Ltd was awarded the franchise for south-west England, previously held by TSW Broadcasting Ltd (winning bid: £7,815,000); and

—GMTV (formerly Sunrise Television) was awarded the franchise for national breakfast-time television, previously held by TV-am plc (winning bid: £34,610,000).

Table 3: Franchise Holders by Region

Area	Company	Winning Bid
East of England	Anglia Television Ltd	£17,804,000
Borders and the Isle of Man	Border Television plc	£52,000
East, west and south Midlands	Central Independent Television plc	£2,000
Channel Islands	Channel Television Ltd	£1,000
North of Scotland	Grampian Television plc	£720,000
North-west England	Granada Television Ltd	£9,000,000
Wales/West of England	HTV Group plc	£20,530,000
London (weekend)	LWT (Holdings) plc	£7,585,000
Central Scotland	Scottish Television plc	£2,000
North-east England	Tyne Tees Television Ltd *	£15,057,000
Northern Ireland	Ulster Television plc	£1,027,000
Yorkshire	Yorkshire Television Ltd *	£37,700,000

* In December 1992 Yorkshire Television and Tyne Tees Television merged to form a single company, Yorkshire–Tyne Tees Television.

Channel 3 licences are awarded for a ten-year period by competitive tender to the highest bidder who has passed a quality threshold. However, in exceptional cases a lower bid can be selected—for instance, where an applicant is able to offer a significantly better quality of service than that offered by the highest bidder.

There are substantial safeguards for quality programming. Licensees are required to offer a diverse programme service, a proportion of good quality programmes, as well as high-quality regional and national news and current affairs programmes, and children's and religious programmes. There is, for the first time, a statutory duty to present programmes made in and about the region. There is also a requirement for district regional programming to be aimed at different areas within regions.

Channel 3 licensees are obliged to operate a national programme network. Networking arrangements are subject to government approval so that anti-competitive practices are avoided.

Independent Television News

A common news service is provided 24 hours a day by Independent Television News (ITN). ITN has been appointed to supply a service of national and international news to the ITV network for a ten-year period starting in January 1993. Under the Broadcasting Act 1990 ITN must widen its share-ownership by 1994 to reduce the controlling ITV shareholders to 49 per cent. From 1993 no company has been allowed to own more than 20 per cent of shares.

The two London broadcasters, Carlton Television and London Weekend Television, run a joint local news and sports operation, London News Network.

Channel 4

Channel 4, which began broadcasting in 1982, provides a national television service throughout Britain, except in Wales, which has a corresponding service—S4C (Sianel Pedwar Cymru—see p. 38). In January 1993 Channel 4 became a statutory corporation, licensed and regulated by the ITC, selling its own advertising time and retaining the proceeds. Previously it had been a limited public company owned by the ITC, and the service, including that in Wales, was financed by annual subscriptions from the former ITV programme companies in return for advertising time in fourth channel programmes broadcast in their own regions.

Channel 4's remit is to provide programme services with a distinctive character and to appeal to tastes and interests not generally catered for by Channel 3. It must present a suitable proportion of educational programmes and encourage innovation and experiment. It commissions programmes from the ITV companies and independent producers and buys programmes in the international markets. Channel 4 broadcasts for approximately 139 hours a week, about half of which are devoted to informative programmes.

S4C

In Wales programmes on the fourth channel are run and controlled by S4C, previously known as the Welsh Fourth Channel Authority. Under the Broadcasting Act 1990, S4C became a broadcaster in its own right. Its members are appointed by the Government.

S4C is required to see that a significant proportion of programming, in practice 23 hours a week, is in the Welsh language and that programmes broadcast between 18.30 and 22.00 hours are mainly in Welsh. At other times S4C transmits national Channel 4 programmes. Like Channel 4, S4C has sold its own advertising time since January 1993. As S4C is expected to cover only 10 per cent of its costs in this way, the remainder is to be financed by the Government.

Sources of ITV and Channel 4 Programmes

Most programmes transmitted on ITV and Channel 4 are made by the ITV companies and ITN or commissioned from independent producers. ITC regulations place a limit on the proportion of non-European material broadcast. At least 86 per cent of all transmissions up to midnight must be from EC sources or be exempted for cultural or educational reasons. After midnight the quota is 75 per cent.

During 1991 transmissions on ITV of new programmes commissioned from independent producers totalled almost 1,400 hours (21 per cent), a rise of 3 per cent on the previous year. By the end of 1992 ITV was committed to reaching a transmitted target of 25 per cent of all new programmes made for the channel (excluding news and news magazines), produced by the independent sector. Since the beginning of 1993 the 25 per cent quota has become a statutory requirement.

Other Recent Developments

The Proposed Channel 5

A new national terrestrial television channel—Channel 5—was advertised in April 1992 and was intended to come into operation in late 1994. The new channel was to be financed through advertising, subscription or sponsorship, or a combination of all three. Owing to limited frequency availability Channel 5 would cover a predicted maximum of 75 per cent of households.

The ten-year licence was to be awarded by competitive tender, with applicants having to pass a quality threshold similar in scope to that for Channel 3. It was intended that the new channel would have similar, though less stringent, programming requirements as apply to Channel 3—news and current affairs, religious and children's programmes, high quality programmes, and a diverse service. However, it would not be required to show either regional or local programmes. The licensee would be required to retune domestic electronic equipment (for example, video cassette recorders) which might suffer interference from Channel 5 transmission.

In December 1992 the ITC announced its decision not to award a licence. It had received only one bid and was not satisfied that the applicant would be able to maintain its proposed service throughout the period of the licence. The ITC is currently reviewing the future options for the Channel 5 licence.

Gaelic TV Fund

The Gaelic Television Committee, appointed by the ITC, was set up under the Broadcasting Act 1990, to administer government funds to finance the making of television programmes in Gaelic. A Gaelic Television Fund of £9.5 million has been created and programmes thus financed came on screen in January 1993. The Fund aims to increase the present output of Gaelic television programmes from 100 to about 300 hours each year. The Fund may also be used to provide training and research.

Local Television

The Broadcasting Act 1990 makes provision for the further development of local television services. Local delivery licences will be awarded by competitive tender but there will be no quality threshold. ITC licence holders will be able to supply national and local television channels using both cable and microwave transmissions systems. Services delivered could include Channel 5 in parts of the country where it would not be available on UHF. Other services could be aimed at communities such as ethnic minorities.

Independent Radio

Local Radio

The Radio Authority is required to ensure that licensed services, taken as a whole, are of a high quality and offer a range of programmes calculated to appeal to a variety of tastes and interests. Powers to deter 'pirate' or illegal broadcasters have been strengthened.

In the course of the 1990s more new stations will come on the air, some of which could be neighbourhood and 'community-of-interest' stations. Areas to be covered will initially be those at present unserved or only marginally served by independent local radio. Local radio licences are not allocated by competitive tender; the success of licence applications is in part determined by the extent to which applicants meet the needs and interests of the people living in the area and whether they have the necessary financial resources to sustain programme plans for the eight-year licence period.

Some of the locations have been selected with small-scale 'community radio' in mind. As part of its brief to develop a wide range of radio services of varying scale and character, the Authority aims to establish a number of stations which will be more specialist in their output than other commercial radio services. The Authority has advertised five regional local licences covering: the North East; the North West; Central Scotland; the West Midlands; and the Severn Estuary. It is looking for applicants who will offer something different from what is already available. The Authority's predecessor, the IBA, began advertising licences for 'community of interest' stations in 1988. Jazz FM became the first of the new London music stations, starting up in 1990.

Restricted Service Licences

Until January 1991 the Home Office dealt with 'special event' licences issued to cover particular events and restricted to the site of the event only. Under the Broadcasting Act 1990 this category of licence has been extended and responsibility for it handed to the

Radio Authority. Unlike full local radio service licences which have to be advertised and competed for, restricted service licences are issued on demand (subject to certain conditions and frequency availability). Licences are usually issued for a maximum of 28 days and for a localised coverage area—for example, part of a city or town, or an arena.

Since January 1991 the Authority has licensed around 490 services. Most of the stations aim to cover specific events, for example, sports events, school and college projects, arts festivals, carnivals, and conferences. Many were used as fund-raising projects for charities, while others operated as trial services with a view to applying for a local radio licence when one is advertised.

Independent National Radio

The Radio Authority is allocating licences by competitive tender to the highest cash bidder for three national commercial radio services.

—The licence for the first independent national radio service—INR1—was awarded to Classic FM in mid-1991. The new station, which plays mainly popular classical music, together with relevant news and information, began broadcasting in September 1992.

—The licence for the second independent national service—INR2—was awarded in early 1992 to Virgin 1215. This station, which began broadcasting in April 1993, plays broad-based rock music.

—The third national service—INR3—will be advertised during

the early part of 1994. It must be a speech-based service, broad-cast on AM.

Cable Services

A cable system is primarily a means of delivering television and radio to the home, although cable operators are increasingly taking advantage of the liberalised telecommunications environment in Britain to provide telephone services as well. Cable services are delivered to consumers through underground cables and paid for by subscription. The cable is connected to viewers' existing television sets usually through a set-top box provided by the cable operator. The television channels carried by cable systems include those from a number of satellites, as well as from other sources. Because a cable connection avoids the need for individual viewers to have satellite dishes, receivers and decoders, cable provides an easy and effective way of delivering the new television and radio choices now developing.

Broadband Cable

'Broadband cable', the cable systems currently being designed and built, can carry between 30 and 45 television channels. They are able to control which channels are delivered to specific premises, allowing viewers receiving cable television to subscribe to some channels but not to others. Franchises have already been granted covering areas which include two-thirds of all homes and nearly all urban areas in Britain, over 14.5 million households in total. Some 57 broadband franchises are now operating. The franchises which have made the most extensive progress are in Croydon, Birmingham, Coventry, Swindon, Aberdeen, Windsor and

Slough, Bristol, Liverpool and parts of London. At present over 2 million homes are able to receive broadband cable services; there are almost 500,000 subscribers. The number of telephone lines installed by cable operators rose fivefold during 1992 to well over 100,000.

Different Kinds of Cable Systems

Broadband cable franchises: These are the multichannel and interactive systems at present being built or planned in most areas of Britain. They are allowed to provide a full range of new television channels, telecommunications services and interactive services.

Local delivery franchises: These are similar to cable franchises, except that the licensee may utilise not only broadband cable but also SMATV (see below) and MVDS. MVDS or 'wireless cable', a technique still under development, has not so far been used in Britain.

Broadcast relay: These systems are often called communal aerial systems and exist to provide BBC, ITV and Channel 4 to a number of homes from a master aerial.

Upgrade systems: These are former broadcast relay systems, often covering large parts of towns, which were upgraded to carry satellite television channels. Most have limited channel capacity and are likely to be replaced eventually by franchised systems.

SMATV (satellite master antenna television): These are smaller systems—often serving only blocks of flats—which have been built to deliver a range of satellite television channels to the homes connected to them.

The *Inspector Morse* series, produced by Central Independent Television, has been sold in nearly 50 countries, reaching an estimated worldwide audience of 750 million.

Channel 4

The ITC's new Code of Programme Sponsorship has offered increased scope for sponsorship on ITV and Channel 4.

The Natural World, a BBC 2 series produced by the world-famous Natural History Unit in Bristol.

Kevin Phillips

An ITN camera crew on location in the Bahamas preparing for underwater photography.

An 'It's Your BBC!' public meeting in Oxford.

A TV debate during the 1992 election campaign—members of the public were invited to form an audience and take part in the discussions.

Classic FM, which began broadcasting in September 1992, had gained an audience of around 4 million listeners by January 1993.

Ken Bruce, a Radio 2 daytime presenter. The network offers easy listening, jazz, big band, light classical, country and folk music interspersed with conversation, comedy and quizzes.

By October 1992 57 cable franchises were operating, with a total of 380,300 subscribers.

Kevin Phillips

Sky Movies Plus is the most popular satellite channel.

BBC Photographs Library

Digital editing of HDTV.

Licences

Until 1991 the cable industry was regulated by the Cable Authority, which was responsible for issuing licences, supervising programme services and promoting cable development. These responsibilities are now carried out by the Cable and Satellite Division of the ITC and by the Radio Authority which issues cable radio licences.

The ITC is continuing the Cable Authority's practice of awarding only one broadband cable franchise in any given area so that the new franchise is protected from direct competition in the early stages.

The ITC grants 15-year franchises on a non-competitive basis to the highest bidder, provided that:

— the system proposed is technically acceptable;

— the service can be funded throughout the period of the franchise;

— the coverage of the area is not substantially less than that proposed by another bidder; and

— the applicant is a fit and proper person to be licensed.

A cable or local delivery licence allows the operator to supply to homes in his or her area a service including any television or radio channel which is itself licensed, together with any acceptable channel originating in another country. The new broadband cable systems carry up to 40 television channels, including terrestrial broadcasts, satellite television, and channels delivered by video-tape. Cable systems usually carry a local channel. Initially these may provide text information but in several areas community television covers local news and events and provides feature programmes of special interest to people in the locality. Interactive services such as home shopping, home banking, security and alarm services, electronic mail and remote meter readings are also possible.

ITC licences are required for systems capable of serving more than 1,000 homes. Systems extending beyond a single building and up to 1,000 homes require only an individual licence from OFTEL.

Systems confined within a single building—such as a block of flats—may operate without any individual licence, even in an area in which otherwise exclusive rights have been granted to a franchisee.

Since January 1991 new operators, and some established ones, have had the choice of using microwave transmissions to extend their coverage beyond viewers who already have cable. Cable investment must be privately financed.

Programme Regulation
Although all cable channels need a licence from the ITC, regulation is as light as possible so as to encourage the development of a wide range of services and facilities, and flexible enough to adapt to changing technology. Cable regulation is different from that imposed on the traditional broadcasting services. Most important, there is no need to ensure that every new cable channel carries a mixture of information, education and entertainment. However, the licensed programmes are obliged not to infringe the ITC's codes on programmes, advertising and sponsorship (see p. 64). If they do so, the ITC can impose fines on the company or, as a last resort, revoke the licence.

Teletext

The BBC and independent television each operates a teletext service, offering constantly updated information on a variety of subjects, including sport, travel, local weather conditions and entertainment. The teletext system allows the television signal to carry additional information which can be selected and displayed as 'pages' of text and graphics on receivers equipped with the necessary decoders. Both the BBC and Channels 3 and 4 services have a subtitling facility for certain programmes for people with hearing difficulties. These services are available whenever the transmitters are on the air. Since April 1992 the BBC Ceefax TV and Radio pages have been produced by a private company, Intelfax.

Nearly 40 per cent of households in Britain have teletext sets and over 7 million people turn to the service daily (more than the circulation figures for most daily newspapers).

Licences

The Broadcasting Act 1990 introduced a new regulatory system for licensing spare capacity within the television signal. This allows more varied use of spare capacity—data transfer, for instance—but the position of teletext and subtitling on commercial television is safeguarded. Channel 3 is obliged to offer a subtitling service for at least 50 per cent of their programmes within 1998, with further increases after that.

At the end of 1991 the ITC advertised three teletext licences—a single public service licence for teletext on Channels 3 and 4 (and S4C) and two separate licences for commercial additional services to subscription or closed user groups, using three lines of spare capacity on each channel. These ten-year licences are awarded by competitive tender, with applicants having to satisfy certain statutory requirements before their cash bid can be considered. The ITC awarded the main teletext licence to Teletext UK Ltd, which replaced Oracle in January 1993, and awarded one of the commercial additional service licences on Channel 3 to the only bidder, Data Broadcasting International; the other commercial additional service licence on Channel 4 remains unallocated.

Direct Broadcasting by Satellite

Direct broadcasting by satellite (DBS), by which television pictures are transmitted directly by satellite into people's homes, has been available throughout Britain since 1989. The signals from satellite broadcasting are receivable using specially designed aerials or 'dishes' and associated reception equipment.

Several British-based satellite television channels have been set up to supply programmes to cable operators and viewers with dishes in Britain and, in some cases, throughout Europe. While some offer general entertainment, others concentrate on specific areas of interest, such as sport, music and children's programmes.

Non-domestic satellite services, such as those on the Astra satellite, use frequencies available for telecommunications, and require a licence from the ITC which, like that for cable-only programmes, imposes no positive obligations but requires conformity with ITC codes. Some 15 per cent of households in Britain are able to receive satellite television, either through cable or through their own dish.

The largest satellite programmer is BSkyB (British Sky Broadcasting), which provides six channels devoted to light entertainment, news, feature films and sport transmitted from the Astra satellite. BSkyB has made substantial progress in establishing Britain's first major television subscription business using its two film channels. By the end of 1991, this was already the second largest in Europe in terms of numbers of subscribers.

Each Astra satellite can transmit 16 channels simultaneously. Two satellites are operational so far, with more planned, and provide about 14 channels in English. In addition to BSkyB, other satellite channels available to British viewers include UK Gold (general entertainment—see below), Eurosport (sport), CNN (news), MTV (pop videos), the Children's Channel (a service for children) and TV Asia (for Asian viewers). The choice available to viewers is expanding steadily.

UK Gold
In November 1992 BBC Enterprises and Thames TV, one of the former ITV franchisees, launched a joint entertainment satellite channel—UK Gold—on the Astra satellite. At present the service, which broadcasts for 20 hours a day, is based on existing programming and draws on the large programme libraries of both companies. Programmes include drama, soaps, comedy, children's television and quizzes. The service is free to all satellite viewers.

Treatment of Certain Subjects

Because broadcasting is an extremely powerful medium with the potential to offend, exploit and cause harm, it is recognised that the traditional editorial independence enjoyed by the broadcasting authorities should be accompanied by responsibilities relating to taste and standard in the content of programmes.

Current Affairs and Political Broadcasting

Although the principle of fair dealing applies to all types of programme, news programmes carry a special weight of responsibility because the public takes most of the information about events from broadcasting. Research conducted at the end of 1990 showed that more than two-thirds of the population regard television as their main source of news.

The ITC and the Radio Authority have a statutory duty to see that, as far as possible, their programmes comply with certain requirements, among them that all news programmes—in whatever form—are presented with accuracy and impartiality, and that impartiality is shown by those presenting programmes on matters of political or industrial controversy or relating to current public policy. Although not subject to such statutory requirements, the BBC recognises similar obligations to treat controversial subjects with due impartiality in the news services and in programmes dealing with matters of public policy. The broadcasting authorities must as a rule refrain from expressing an opinion on matters of public policy.

Parliamentary Broadcasting

Both the BBC and the independent broadcasting companies provide programmes on current parliamentary issues and political topics. Under its licence the BBC is required, when Parliament is in session, to broadcast an impartial, day-by-day account—prepared by professional reporters—of the proceedings of both Houses of Parliament: this is the Radio 4 programme *Today in Parliament.* Radio 4 also broadcasts *Yesterday in Parliament*; *In Committee*, a weekly programme on the work of select committees on departmental affairs; and *The Week in Westminster*, which invites Members of Parliament to comment on the week's parliamentary affairs. On television, BBC 2 broadcasts *Scrutiny*, a weekly programme on the work of committees. On Tuesdays, Wednesdays and Thursdays BBC 2 broadcasts *Westminster Live* from the House of Commons. Channel 4 broadcasts *The Parliament Programme* on weekday afternoons. Weekly programmes on parliamentary affairs are broadcast by BBC regional television and a number of independent local radio stations. The broadcasters have editorial control of all these programmes.

The proceedings of both Houses of Parliament may be broadcast on television and radio, either live, or more usually in recorded and edited form on news and current affairs programmes. Radio broadcasting of some of the proceedings of both Houses of Parliament began in 1978. Proceedings of the House of Lords have been televised since 1985; those of the House of Commons since 1989.

Special proceedings are broadcast live—for example, the presentation of the Budget by the Chancellor of the Exchequer or Prime Minister's Question Time on important occasions.

Political Broadcasting

The Government has no general privileged access to radio or television; government announcements of major importance naturally find a place in scheduled news bulletins as matters of news interest but broadcasting authorities enjoy complete editorial independence.

Certain broadcasts are subject to an agreement between the political parties and the broadcasters. These include ministerial and party political broadcasts.

Ministerial Broadcasts

The Government has the right to broadcast on radio and television from time to time because of its executive responsibilities. Such broadcasts fall into two categories:

1 Broadcasts in which ministers explain legislation or administrative policies approved by Parliament, or seek the public's co-operation in matters where there is a consensus of opinion. There is no right of reply by the Opposition to these broadcasts, neither are they transmitted by independent television as a matter of course although they may be broadcast on particular occasions.

2 Occasions when the Prime Minister or another minister broadcasts to the nation on matters of great national or international importance—for example, the broadcast made by the Prime Minister, John Major, in January 1991 on the outbreak of the Gulf War. In these cases the Opposition is entitled to claim a right of reply. Once the Opposition has exercised this right the BBC and independent television arrange additional broadcast discussions of the issues, in which any party with electoral support comparable with that of the Liberal Democrats (the third

largest party in the House of Commons) is entitled to be represented, together with the two main parties. Like the BBC, independent television is bound to transmit a third discussion programme once it has shown the first two. None of the broadcasts need be shown simultaneously on both services.

On the evening of the day of the Budget speech in Parliament the Chancellor of the Exchequer appears on both BBC and independent television to explain the proposals to the nation. On the following evening a leading member of the Opposition is automatically given a similar length of time on the air to reply. The Liberal Democrats also have an opportunity to broadcast the next day.

Party Political Broadcasts
The broadcasters allocate time to each of the political parties represented in Parliament for an annual series of party political broadcasts. The number of broadcasts for each party is based on the votes cast at the previous general election. These broadcasts are under the editorial control of the political parties and are arranged in two series: one on television and the other on radio. The broadcasts are also shown on ITV and BSkyB. In addition to the series of national network broadcasts, the Scottish and Welsh national and Northern Ireland parties are allocated party political broadcasts in their respective countries.

When a general election is announced the regular series of party political broadcasts is ended. Arrangements for party election broadcasts during general elections are made by a committee consisting of representatives of the political parties, the BBC, the ITC, the ITV Network Centre (the trade association for the ITV companies), S4C and the Radio Authority.

The allocation of party election broadcasts for the April 1992 general election gave the Conservative and Labour parties five national television broadcasts each, and the Liberal Democrats four. The Scottish National Party, Plaid Cymru and the Northern Ireland parties were allocated broadcasts in Scotland, Wales and Northern Ireland respectively. The Green Party and the Natural Law Party each qualified for one broadcast because they were contesting more than 50 seats (out of 651). All the parties mentioned above were also allocated radio time. In all such broadcasts editorial control rests with the parties.

During the build-up to an election extended news programmes cover all aspects of the major parties' campaigns at national level and in the constituencies. Special election programmes include discussions between politicians from the rival parties; often a studio audience of members of the public may challenge and question senior politicians. Radio phone-ins also allow ordinary callers to question, or put their views to, political leaders. Broadcast coverage also includes interviews with leading figures from all the parties and reports focusing on particular election issues, and commentaries from political journalists.

Candidates may take part in an election campaign programme about their constituency only if all their rival candidates take part or agree that the programme may go ahead without their presence.

The use of transmitting stations outside Britain for election propaganda is prohibited unless the arrangements are made with the public bodies responsible for broadcasting (or a programme contractor).

Educational Broadcasting

Both the BBC and Channel 4 broadcast programmes for schools and also Continuing Education programmes aimed at adults.

Educational broadcasts differ from the educative programmes of the general output in that they aim to help viewers or listeners acquire understanding of a body of knowledge, gain a skill or qualification, or motivate them to take up further learning opportunities. The broadcasts form part of a continuing learning experience often supported by non-broadcast materials and activities.

Broadcasting for Schools

Broadcasts to schools deal with most subjects of the national curriculum, while education programmes for adults cover many areas of learning and vocational training. Supporting material, in the form of books, pamphlets, filmstrips, computer software, and audio and video cassettes, is available to supplement the programmes. Around 90 per cent of primary schools and 93 per cent of secondary schools in Britain use schools television.

A key problem of educational broadcasting is the need to ensure a close relationship between broadcasters and educational interests. For the BBC, the Education Broadcasting Council for the United Kingdom consists of representatives appointed by the main educational organisations and experts appointed by the BBC. It advises the BBC on educational broadcasting policy.

The Council works through three programme committees which among them concentrate on primary, secondary and continuing education; most committee members are practising teachers. The Council holds regular meetings of specialist panels and convenes panels or conferences to give guidance on particular issues. Some 18 full-time education officers are employed; 11 of these are schools specialists, who visit schools to judge how effective the programmes have been and advise on how best to use the broadcasts and accompanying publications. For BBC local radio there are local panels, with an interest in both school and adult education, over which the Council exercises general supervision.

Separate Education Broadcasting Councils for Scotland, Wales and Northern Ireland are represented on the main Council.

BBC Radio 5

The introduction of Radio 5 in 1990 (see p. 26) provided the BBC's Schools, Children's and Youth Programmes Department with new opportunities to add variety to their output, which now includes for the first time the production of programmes for evening listening.

The daily morning sequence on the network covers a range of subjects for primary and secondary schools, with the emphasis on the expressive arts (movement, music, drama and poetry) and modern languages. A major innovation in 1990–91 was the introduction of *Curriculum Resources*, a daily programme backed by teaching packs to support subject-based or cross-curricular teaching and learning. Schools, Children's and Youth Programmes now provides stories, drama and features for children and young people in their own time at home. In the evening Radio 5 offers readings and plays, introducing a new generation to world literature—450 hours a year of drama and stories; almost all under half an hour in length—and features output reflecting listeners' interests in sports, the arts, fashion and music, while giving them access to air their views.

The ITC

The ITC is advised on the educational output of its programme contractors by its Education Advisory Council. Members are appointed by the ITC. The production teams of the programme companies are advised by special committees whose members keep in close contact with schools and other educational interests in their regions. Regular consultations take place with the BBC to ensure that duplication of provision is avoided as far as possible.

Schools programmes supplied by the ITV companies have been broadcast on Channel 4 since 1987. The 1990 Broadcasting Act requires the ITC to do all it can to secure a programme service that meets the needs of schools in Britain. In January 1993 Channel 4 assumed responsibility for commissioning independent television schools programmes and managing both planning and schedules. Under the new system about half of the commissioned productions are placed with a consortium owned by many of the companies formerly responsible for the ITV schools service. The consortium has set up the Educational Television Company to make schools broadcasts and fulfil on behalf of Channel 4 the role of supplying information and liaison. The remainder of the commissioning can go to a variety of bodies, such as new companies, ITC licensees who are not members of the consortium, and the BBC. In addition, a network of nine education officers throughout the regions is being set up, working not for separate ITV companies as before, but as a unified team under Channel 4.

Continuing Education

Education programmes for adults form an important part of the output of both the BBC and Channel 4. In 1991–92 the BBC provided more than 600 hours of radio and 250 hours of television for people interested in continuing education. Many of the programmes are supported by books and pamphlets, and some by telephone helplines.

With the introduction of Radio 5 , the Continuing Education department of the BBC has now moved into live magazine programmes, covering issues such as parenthood and health.

Continuing Education and Training Television concentrates on work, business and training; languages; basic skills and education; and basic science and information technology. Series in 1990–91 included those preparing viewers for the European single market; dealing with companies in Eastern and Western Europe; and the Japanese language. The 1991–92 series included 'Play it Safe'—a prime-time child accident prevention campaign—and the Training Hour was launched on Sunday mornings.

The BBC recently completed a major basic skills accreditation scheme in partnership with the Adult Basic Skills Unit of the Department for Education and with the Department of Employment. Many students are now receiving their first certificates at the 650 learning centres throughout Britain. In March 1992 the BBC worked with the Employment Department, and the organisers of National Adult Learning Week on a major 'second chance' initiative. This involved producing 15 short comedy sketches for BBC 1 and resulted in 57,000 people telephoning a national helpline for advice on education and training opportunities for adults.

The Open University

The BBC broadcasts television and radio programmes made specially for the Open University. The Open University is an independent autonomous university, which exists to provide the opportunity for higher education, by distance-learning, to every adult resident in Britain. The University's main teaching methods consist of correspondence work; regular viewing of, and listening to, television and radio programmes; contact with counsellors and tutors; and written examinations and assignments.

The BBC broadcasts around three hours of radio time and 22 hours of television time each week on behalf of the Open University.

Support for the Arts

Both BBC radio and television and the independent companies broadcast a wide variety of drama (including adaptations of novels and stage plays), opera, ballet, and music as well as general arts magazine programmes and documentaries. These have won many international awards at festivals such as the Prix Italia and Montreux International Television Festivals. ITV companies also make grants for arts promotion in their regions.

Broadcasting is thus a major medium for making the arts available to the general public and is a crucial source of work for actors, musicians, writers, composers, technicians and others in the arts world. It has created its own forms—nothing like arts documentaries or drama series, for instance, exist in any other medium. Broadcasters commission and produce a vast quantity of new work, notably, but not confined to music and drama; a playwright or poet can reach a much larger audience through radio or television than through live performances. Television and radio provide critical debate, information and education about the arts.

Surveys have shown repeatedly that television is the most important medium for finding out about and stimulating an interest in the arts. In addition, through listings programmes, television helps to market the arts.

Drama

The BBC Radio Drama Department, which produces 300 new plays each year and has an annual listening audience in Britain and overseas (through the BBC World Service) of nearly 500 million, is the largest single patron of original drama in the world. At least one play a week is transmitted on either Radio 3 or Radio 4, while the BBC World Service also broadcasts 52 plays a year.

The Radio Drama Department receives some 10,000 manuscripts each year; 6,000 to 7,000 are unsolicited. Half of the Department's producers are based outside London and are responsible for a number of distinctive regional productions coming from Northern Ireland, Scotland and Wales. Radio 4 devotes two weeks of its drama schedules each year to writers new to radio aged between 15 and 30.

Music

The BBC has five orchestras, which employ many of Britain's full-time professional musicians. Each week it broadcasts about 100 hours of classical and other music (both live and recorded) on its Radio 3 FM channel. BBC Radio 1 broadcasts rock and pop music 24 hours a day, and a large part of the output of BBC Radio 2 and of many independent local radio stations is popular and light music.

The BBC regularly commissions new music, particularly by British composers, and sponsors concerts, competitions and festivals. Each summer it presents and broadcasts the BBC Promenade Concerts (the 'Proms') at the Royal Albert Hall.

The first of the three new independent national radio stations (see p. 42)—Classic FM—broadcasts mainly popular classical music; the second—Virgin 1215—plays broad-based rock.

Film

In the last ten years Channel 4, with its 'Film on Four' series, and more recently the BBC have proved a vitally important source of production finance for the British film industry. Since its establishment in 1982 Film on Four has funded some 180 features. These have included films dealing with ethnic and sexual minorities; art films; co-productions set in Europe and the developing countries; and films produced by workshops and in the regions. Films have included *My Beautiful Launderette*, *Mona Lisa*, *Prick Up Your Ears*, *Hope and Glory*, *Moonlighting* and *The Draughtsman's Contract*. Most of the Film on Four productions have received between 30 and 80 per cent of their funding from Channel 4.

Animation

The recent resurgence of interest in the cartoon film in Britain is due in great part to the pioneering work of British animators who have created 3D animation and computer animation. The acceptance of animation as mainstream television viewing is due largely to the commissioning policies of Channel 4 and S4C which have a combined investment in animation of £2 million to £3 million a year. Both channels have proved an important source of production finance, commissioning animated films for adult audiences and has fostered the work of Nick Park, Peter Lord, David Sproxton, Tim Burton and John Lasseter. Two British films, *Creature Comforts* by Aardman Animation and *Manipulation* directed by Daniel Greaves, won Oscars in 1991 and 1992 respectively.

BBC and S4C have collaborated on the production of cartoon versions of six of Shakespeare's plays, which began screening in autumn 1992. *Shakespeare: The Animated Tales* were made in

Russia by the animation studio Soyuzmultfilm, using a variety of animation techniques.

The ITV Fund

ITV provides financial support for the arts in two ways: nationally from all the ITV companies acting together through the ITV Fund, which accounts for 44 per cent of the total donated, and locally by each individual company in support of organisations within their own region. In 1991 ITV Fund grants were made to, among others, the National Museum of Photography, Film and Television; the British Television Institute and the National Film Archive; the National Film and Television School; the Actors' Centre; and the London College of Music. Grants are given to organisations which are nationwide in scope and likely to improve or maintain the quality of programmes on television.

The ITV Fund is also responsible for the Regional Theatre Directors Scheme, the only scheme of its kind in Britain, which each year awards grants for training young theatre directors.

Special Aspects of Broadcasting

Summarised below are some special aspects of broadcasting. These include broadcasting standards; advertising; copyright; audience research; recent technical developments; and relations between the British broadcasting authorities and broadcasting organisations overseas.

Broadcasting Standards

The independence enjoyed by the broadcasting authorities carries with it certain obligations over programmes and programme content. Programmes must display, as far as possible, a proper balance and wide range of subject matter, impartiality in matters of controversy and accuracy in news coverage, and must not offend against good taste. Broadcasters must also comply with legislation relating to obscenity and incitement to racial hatred.

The BBC and the other regulatory authorities apply codes providing guidance on violence and standards of taste and decency in television programmes, particularly during hours when children are likely to be viewing.

Under the 1990 Broadcasting Act the Government can proscribe unacceptable foreign satellite services receivable in Britain. Anyone in Britain supporting such a service can now be prosecuted for a criminal offence.

Programme Codes

The ITC operates statutory codes of practice governing television programmes. They cover:

—impartiality;

—the portrayal of violence;

—causing offence;

—privacy;

—gathering of information;

—party political and parliamentary broadcasting;

—terrorism;

—crime; and

—communication with the public.

The codes apply to all services licensed by the ITC and to certain foreign satellite programmes included in local delivery services licensed by the ITC. The ITC can impose sanctions, including fines, on licensees who breach the statutory codes.

The Radio Authority has published broadly similar programme codes and handles complaints against licensees who are alleged to have breached these codes. It also publishes a quarterly complaints bulletin.

Broadcasting Standards Council

The Broadcasting Standards Council (BSC) was set up by the Government in 1988 to act as a focus for public concern about the portrayal of violence and sex, and about standards of taste and decency. Its remit covers television and radio programmes and broadcast advertisements, and includes monitoring programmes broadcast into Britain from abroad. The BSC has drawn up a code of practice on these matters. Under the Broadcasting Act 1990 the BSC has been granted statutory powers which require the codes of practice of the BBC and other broadcasting regulatory bodies to reflect the BSC's own code.

The BSC monitors programmes, examines complaints from the public and undertakes research. Complaints about television must normally be made within two months, and those about radio within three weeks, of the date on which the programme concerned was last broadcast. The BSC may decide to hold a hearing to consider a complaint and can require a summary of the complaint and of its findings to be broadcast and to be published in writing. It has already published the results of several public attitude surveys.

During April 1991–92 the BSC received 2,662 complaints, of which 1,130 fell within its remit. Of these, 898 were about specific programmes or advertisements and the Council reached a finding about 644 of them. Ninety-seven of the complaints were under consideration at the end of this period. All the findings were published in the Council's monthly Complaints Bulletin.

Advertising

Independent Television

Advertisements on independent television are broadcast in between programmes as well as in breaks during programmes. Advertisers are not allowed directly to influence programme content or editorial control. Advertisements must be clearly distinguishable and separate from programmes. The time given to them must not be so great as to detract from the value of the programmes as a medium of information, education or entertainment.

Television advertising is limited to an average of seven minutes an hour throughout the day and seven and a half minutes in the peak evening viewing period. On satellite and cable channels the limit is an average of nine minutes each hour over the day. There are also strict limits on the frequency and length of advertising breaks in different types of programmes. There are some categories of programme in which no advertising is permitted, for example, religious services and broadcasts to schools. Independent television's teletext service, Teletext UK Ltd (see p. 47), carries paginated advertisements.

Codes of Practice

The ITC and the Radio Authority are required to operate codes governing standards and practice in advertising, and to give guidance on the types and methods of advertisement which are prohibited. The main aims of the codes are to ensure that advertising:

—is not misleading;

—does not encourage or condone harmful behaviour; and

—does not cause widespread or exceptional offence.

The ITC and the Radio Authority require the companies which they license to comply with the codes. The companies are expected to have adequate procedures to check carefully all advertising proposals before accepting them for transmission. In particular they should ensure that any claims are true, if necessary by inspecting documentary evidence or seeking the advice of independent consultants. These requirements are more rigorous than those applied to any other advertising medium and help to ensure that, as far as possible, commercials appearing on television and radio meet the necessary standards. The ITC codes are kept under regular review with the help of an independent advisory committee comprising representatives of both consumer and advertising interests. The Radio Authority consults widely when changes are made to its codes, but they are not regularly monitored.

Prohibited advertising includes political advertising, betting and advertisements for cigarettes and cigarette tobacco and—on television only—cigars and pipe tobacco. (Advertisements for the last two are permitted on radio.) Since January 1993 Channels 3 and 4 have been allowed to screen religious advertisements provided they comply with the guidelines issued by the ITC. Religious advertising is permitted on radio but must comply with the Radio Authority's code on religious advertising, which prohibits advertisements which seek to recruit members.

The ITC and the Radio Authority can impose severe penalties on any television or radio company failing to comply with their codes. The Broadcasting Standards Council's code of practice (see p. 64) covers advertisements.

Food manufacturers and retailers form the largest category of advertisers. Local advertisers publicise events of local interest, job vacancies and goods on sale in local stores.

The ITC considers all complaints received about television advertising and if it concludes that an investigation is necessary, the television company concerned must submit background material and evidence promptly. All complainants receive a personal reply, and the ITC and Radio Authority each publishes a monthly report summarising the outcome of their investigations. In 1992 the ITC dealt with 3,504 complaints about advertising on television (including teletext, satellite and cable services). In 1992 the Radio Authority received 315 complaints about programming and advertising. Of these, 40 advertising complaints were upheld.

BBC

Under the terms of its Licence and Agreement the BBC must have the consent of the Secretary of State for National Heritage before broadcasting any commercial advertisement. It may not broadcast any sponsored programme. The policy of the BBC is to avoid giving any publicity to any firm or organised interest except when this is necessary in providing effective and informative programmes. It does, however, cover sponsored sporting and artistic events.

A report published by the Monopolies and Mergers Commission in 1992 found that the BBC had gone too far with some of its self-promotions and recommended that it restrict its promotion of BBC goods, on BBC TV, to stills, not moving trails. The recommendation has since been implemented.

Sponsorship

In Britain sponsorship is a relatively new way of helping to finance commercial television and radio programmes although the practice has long been established in other countries. In return for their financial contribution, sponsors receive a credit associating them with a particular programme. The ITC Code of Programme Sponsorship and the Radio Authority's Advertising and Sponsorship Code aim to ensure that sponsors do not exert influence on the editorial content of programmes and that sponsorships are made clear to viewers. The practice known as product placement—the gratuitous mention or showing of brand names—is prohibited in any programme, whether sponsored or not.

News and current affairs programmes on television or radio may not be sponsored in any circumstances and potential sponsors for other categories of programme may be debarred if their involvement could constrain in any way the editorial independence of the programme maker. References to sponsors or their products have to be confined to the beginning and end of a programme and around commercial breaks; they must not appear in the programme itself. All commercial radio programmes other than news bulletins may be sponsored.

Government Publicity

Government publicity material to support non-political campaigns may be broadcast on independent television and radio. This is paid for on a normal commercial basis. Short public service items about health, safety and welfare are also produced by the Central Office of Information for free transmission by the BBC and independent television and radio.

A private sector company, Worldwide Television News (WTN—see p. 79), produces a daily international satellite news service for the Foreign & Commonwealth Office. The service— British Satellite News (BSN)—for which the Foreign & Commonwealth Office has editorial control, transmits news programmes five days a week. These are distributed free of charge by satellite to television stations throughout Eastern Europe, the Middle East and Southern Africa for their use in news bulletins.

Broadcasting and Copyright

All British television and radio broadcasting organisations and many foreign ones are granted copyright in their broadcasts under the Copyright, Designs and Patents Act 1988. Copyright in broadcasts and cable programmes lasts for 50 years from the year of broadcast. Copyright restricts re-broadcasting of the programme or making films or recordings of it (other than for 'timeshifting'—that is, playing back programmes previously recorded off air for private and domestic use). It also restricts permitting a paying audience to see or hear it, either live or recorded.

In addition to the broadcasters' copyright in their own broadcasts, a broadcast may include works which are themselves protected by copyright. These may be literary, dramatic, musical or artistic works, which are protected until 50 years after the death of the author or composer. Films or sound recordings which are protected for 50 years from release may also be included. The broadcasting organisation obtains authorisation from the owner of the copyright in each work included in a broadcast. Performers are similarly protected, and it is an offence knowingly to broadcast a recording of a dramatic, musical or variety act performance or a reading of a literary work without sufficient consent.

Broadcasting organisations are granted a licence to broadcast copyright music by the Performing Right Society, which collectively exercises the composers' rights and distributes the royalties to those whose works are involved. Likewise Phonographic Performance Ltd collectively licenses the broadcasting of sound recordings and distributes the royalties to its constituent recording companies and representatives of the performer. The broadcasting of other copyright works is usually subject to individual agreements.

The Copyright Tribunal has the power to settle any disputes over licensing where a licensing scheme is operated by a collecting society.

There are certain exceptions to copyright which allow copyright material to be used without permission where it is reasonable to do so and where the economic interests of the copyright owner are not damaged. In the context of broadcasting it is not an infringement of copyright to use a work, other than a photograph, for the purposes of news reporting, or any other work, provided there is sufficient acknowledgment, for the purposes of criticism or review.

Audience Research

Both the BBC and the independent sector are required to keep themselves informed on the state of public opinion about the programmes and advertising they broadcast. This is done through the continuous measurement of the size and composition of audiences and their opinions of programmes.

Television

For television, audience research is undertaken through BARB (the Broadcasters' Audience Research Board), which is owned jointly by the BBC and the ITV Network Centre. For independent broadcasting, measuring the size of an audience is very important: the revenue of programme companies depends on their being able to assure advertisers that their programmes are being watched; for the BBC, audience satisfaction is an important component of its public service remit.

Estimates of the number of viewers of television programmes throughout Britain are supplied weekly for BARB by two independent research companies—AGB Research and RSMB Television Research. Automatic electronic meters are fixed to television sets in a representative sample of 4,500 homes to record minute by minute the time during which sets are switched on and the channels to which they are tuned. The sample audience provides further data by recording what they are viewing through a handset on which they also record details about themselves so that the composition of the audience can be discovered.

BARB's measurement of television audiences was improved in 1991 when for the first time both satellite channel viewing—whether on cable or by dish—and the viewing of video-recorded programmes were incorporated. In addition, the published programme figures now reflect the age and sex of visitors who watch television in a BARB panellist's home.

Audience reaction to television programmes is regularly monitored for BARB by the BBC-run Television Opinion Panel. This consists of 3,000 people nationally, aged 12 and over, who each week complete a booklet rating all the programmes they watch on a six-point scale in terms of interest and enjoyment. Regional and children's panels provide equivalent information.

TV Audience Share: January–May 1993

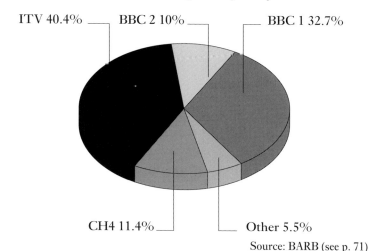

ITV 40.4%   BBC 2 10%   BBC 1 32.7%

CH4 11.4%   Other 5.5%

Source: BARB (see p. 71)

Radio

Until 1992 audiences for BBC radio and for commercial radio were measured separately. In view of the new independent national radio stations (see p. 42), a joint measuring system, known as RAJAR

(Radio Joint Audience Research), was developed and started in late 1992. The contract is held by Research Services Ltd, and measuring takes the form of a seven-day diary, with a different panel of diarists each week recording all programmes listened to on any local or national stations available to them. At present a meter technique is not considered feasible in view of the wide range of radio receivers. As with television programmes, audience reaction to BBC nationally networked radio programmes is monitored by a Listening Panel, consisting of 3,000 listeners aged 12 and over.

Both the BBC and the independent sector conduct regular surveys to gauge audience opinion on television and radio services. Public opinion is further assessed by the BBC and ITC through the work of their advisory committees, councils and panels. Regular public meetings are also held to debate services, and careful consideration

Radio Audience Share: 21 September – 20 December 1992

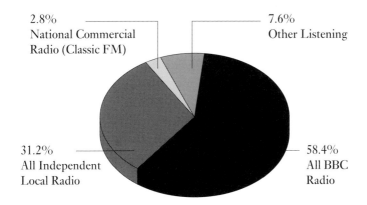

2.8%
National Commercial
Radio (Classic FM)

7.6%
Other Listening

31.2%
All Independent
Local Radio

58.4%
All BBC
Radio

Source: RAJAR (see above)

National Radio Stations – Weekly Audience Reach
21 September – 20 December 1992

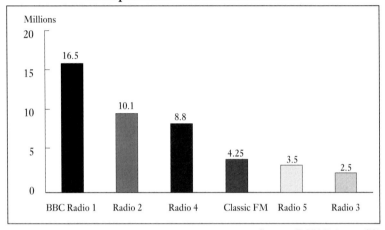

Source: RAJAR (see p. 73)

is given to letters and telephone calls from listeners and viewers. When advertising local radio licences, the Radio Authority invites comments from the public about the radio needs of the area.

Technical Developments

One of the most important recent developments in television has been in news coverage, where compact electronic cameras have replaced film cameras, eliminating the need for film processing and enabling pictures to be transmitted directly to a studio or recorded on video tape on location.

Other recent advances in television broadcasting include:

—adoption of digital video tape recorders;

—increasing use of computer-aided digital equipment for picture generation and manipulation;

—use of portable satellite links to transmit pictures from remote locations to studios; and

—the introduction of stereo sound using the NICAM 728 digital system, developed by the BBC.

Both the independent sector and the BBC are further developing digital techniques for studio applications and inter-studio links; in early 1993 such digital links began operating in the independent sector.

The BBC and the IBA co-operated in the development of teletext, and teletext sets in 30 countries are based on the British system.

In satellite broadcasting the MAC transmission format was developed by IBA engineers, who went on to devise refinements for the MAC system compatible with widescreen television.

Both the BBC and the ITC are undertaking a number of important areas of long-term research.

High-definition Television

Work is being undertaken on the development of a 1250-line wide-screen system (high-definition television—HDTV) for the mid-nineties and beyond. Originally research was carried out under the EUREKA 95 project, and now more widely in other European collaborations. More than 60 European organisations from 13 countries are participating in EUREKA 95. Among other work, NTL (see p. 9) is leading the key group concerned with satellite transmission of the HDTV signal, and the BBC is leading the group responsible for developing the multi-channel digital sound system that will be used.

Enhancements to the PAL Colour Television System

PALplus will bring better quality, clearer, sharper pictures—suitable for a new generation of widescreen televisions—from the mid-1990s onwards. The BBC, the ITC and NTL are contributing to the work of PALplus, a collaborative venture between industry and several European broadcasters.

Digital Terrestrial Television Broadcasting

In the long-term, new developments could allow digital signals to be broadcast within the present UHF television transmission bands. These could well be used to further enhance the quality of existing services, perhaps making possible the introduction of terrestrial HDTV. The key British project in this area is the ITC's SPECTRE system which was begun in 1989. More recently the ITC and the BBC have become involved in European initiatives that aim to advance this type of research on an international basis.

Data Transmission Studies

Work is in progress to develop an 'audio description' service of benefit to visually handicapped viewers. This could take the form of an additional sound channel to be used for a commentary describing the visual content of television programmes. The ITC is leading research in this area within a European Commission-backed consortium known as AUDETEL.

Digital Audio Broadcasting

In 1992 the Government announced support for the introduction of digital audio broadcasting (DAB). The new technology is expected to deliver more services, offering greater choice for listeners, while improving the quality of reception and allowing national services to be transmitted on single frequency networks. In February 1993 the establishment of a National DAB Forum was announced. This will promote plans for introducing DAB and co-ordinate the interests of broadcasters, manufacturers, retailers, service providers and other interested parties. DAB broadcasting is expected to start during 1995.

International Relations

Co-operation between governments on international broadcasting takes place within the Council of Europe (linking 23 countries) and the European Community (comprising 12 member states).

The advent of cable and satellite television in the 1980s provided technical opportunities for cross-border broadcasters to offer European viewers a much wider choice of channels. However, different national regulations on such matters as the length, timing and content of advertising, have inhibited growth of competition in some areas.

In 1991 Britain implemented two important European agreements on cross-border broadcasting: the European Community Directive on Broadcasting and the Council of Europe Convention on Transfrontier Television. Under these, countries have to remove restrictions on the retransmission of programmes originating from other participating countries. They must also ensure that their own broadcasters observe certain minimum standards on advertising and sponsorship, taste and decency and the portrayal of sex and violence on television. Programmes must not be indecent, contain pornography, give undue prominence to violence or be likely to incite racial hatred. Nor should programmes unsuitable for children be broadcast at a time when they are likely to be watching.

European Broadcasting Union

The BBC and the Radio Authority are members of the European Broadcasting Union, which manages Eurovision, the international network of television news and programme exchange. The Union is responsible for the technical and administrative arrangements for co-ordinating the exchange of programme and news over the Eurovision network and intercontinental satellite links. It also maintains a technical monitoring station where frequency measurements and other observations on broadcasting stations are carried out. The Union provides a forum linking the major public services and national broadcasters of Western Europe and other parts of the world, and co-ordinates joint operations in radio and television.

International Telecommunications Union

The BBC takes part in pthe work of the International Telecommunications Union, the United Nations agency responsible for regulating and controlling all international telecommunication services, including radio and television. The Union also allocates and registers all radio frequencies, and promotes and co-ordinates the international study of technical problems in broadcasting.

Other International Bodies

The BBC is an associate member of the Asia–Pacific Broadcasting Union, and also belongs to the Commonwealth Broadcasting Association, whose members meet every two years to discuss public service broadcasting issues.

News Agencies

Britain is a partner in Visnews, the largest television news agency in the world. Visnews supplies world news pictures to over 650 broadcasters in 84 countries and runs a network of bureaux in major cities throughout the world. Reuters is the majority shareholder of the company.

Worldwide Television News, owned by ITN, the American Broadcasting Corporation (ABC) and Channel 9 in Australia, supplies news and a wide range of television services to some 1,000 broadcasters in 93 countries, as well as to governments and international corporations.

Both agencies provide services through the Eurovision network and by satellite.

Training

The BBC provides some non-financial technical assistance, particularly in training the staff of overseas broadcasting organisations. The Government finances overseas students on broadcasting training courses at the BBC, the British Council and the Thomson Foundation.

The Foundation not only provides training in Britain but also conducts courses overseas in broadcast journalism, media management, radio and television production and technology.

Addresses

Central Offices

Department of National Heritage, 2–4 Cockspur Street, London SW1Y 5BQ.

BBC Corporate Headquarters and BBC Radio, Broadcasting House, Portland Place, London W1A 1AA.

BBC Television, Television Centre, Wood Lane, London W12 7RJ.

BBC World Service, PO Box 76, Bush House, London WC2B 4PH.

Broadcasting Complaints Commission, Grosvenor Gardens House, 35–37 Grosvenor Gardens, London SW1 0BS.

Broadcasting Standards Council, 5–8 The Sanctuary, London SW1P 3JS.

Channel 4 Television Company, 60 Charlotte Street, London W1P 2AX.

S4C, Parc Ty Glas, Llanishen, Cardiff CFH 5DU.

Independent Television Commission, 33 Foley Street, London W1P 7LB.

Radio Authority, Holbrook House, 14 Great Queen Street, London WC2B 5DG.

Gaelic Television Committee, 4 Harbour View, Cromwells Quay, Stornoway, Isle of Lewis, PA87 2DF.

ITV Network Centre, Knighton House, 56 Mortimer Street, London W1N 8AN.

BBC National and Regional Offices

BBC Scotland, Broadcasting House, Queen Margaret Drive, Glasgow G12 8DG.

BBC Wales, Broadcasting House, Llantrisant Road, Llandaff, Cardiff CF5 2YQ.

BBC Northern Ireland, Broadcasting House, Ormeau Avenue, Belfast BT2 8HQ.

BBC North, New Broadcasting House, Oxford Road, Manchester M60 1SJ.

BBC Midlands and East, Broadcasting Centre, Pebble Mill, Birmingham B5 7QQ.

BBC South, Broadcasting House, Whiteladies Road, Bristol BS8 2LR.

Independent Television Programme Companies

Anglia Television, Anglia House, Norwich NR1 1JG.

Border Television, The Television Centre, Carlisle CA1 3NT.

Carlton Television, 101 St Martin's Lane, London WC2 4AZ.

Central Independent Television, Central House, Broad Street, Birmingham B1 2JP.

Channel Television, The Television Centre, St Helier, Jersey, Channel Islands.

GMTV, The London Television Centre, London SE1 9LT.

Grampian Television, Queen's Cross, Aberdeen AB9 2XJ.

Granada Television, Granada Television Centre, Manchester M60 9EA.

HTV Wales, The Television Centre, Culverhouse Cross, Cardiff CF5 6XJ.

HTV West, The Television Centre, Bath Road, Bristol BS4 3HG.

London Weekend Television (LWT), South Bank Television Centre, London SE1 9LT.

Meridian Broadcasting, Television Centre, Southampton SO9 5HZ.

Scottish Television, Cowcaddens, Glasgow G2 3PR.

Ulster Television, Havelock House, Ormeau Road, Belfast BT7 1EB.

Westcountry Television, Western Wood Way, Language Science Park, Plymouth PL7 5BG.

Yorkshire–Tyne Tees Television, Television Centre, Leeds LS3 1JS.

Independent National Radio

Classic FM, Academic House, 24–28 Oval Road, London NW1 7DQ.

Virgin 1215, 1 Golden Square, London W1R 4DJ.

Other

Independent Television News (ITN), 200 Gray's Inn Road, London WC1X 8XZ.

London News Network, The London Television Centre, Upper Ground, London SE1 9LT.

British Sky Broadcasting, 6 Centaurs Business Park, Grant Way, Isleworth, Middlesex TW7 5QD.

Further Reading

Official Publications   £

Broadcasting Act 1990.
ISBN 0 10 544290 9.   HMSO   1990   15.60

*Broadcasting in the '90s: Competition, Choice
and Quality. The Government's Plans for
Broadcasting Legislation.*
Home Office. Cm 517.
ISBN 0 10 105072 7.   HMSO   1988   7.20

*British Broadcasting 1922–1982: A Selected
and Annotated Bibliography.*
ISBN 0 946358 14 1.   BBC Data Publications   1983   15.00

*Enquiry into Standards of Cross-Media
Promotion: Report to the Secretary of State for
Trade and Industry.* Cm 1436.
ISBN 0 10 114362 1.   HMSO   1991   12.60

*Extending Choice: The BBC's Role in the New
Broadcasting Age.*
ISBN 0 563 36903 5.   BBC   1992   2.95

*The Future of the BBC: A Consultation
Document.* Cm 2098.
ISBN 0 10 120982 7.   HMSO   1992   7.10

£

The Future of Broadcasting. Third Report of the
House of Commons Home Affairs Committee, Session 1987-88.
Vol 1. Report, together with the Proceedings of the
Committee.
ISBN 0 10 296688 1.   HMSO   1988   6.90

Vol 2. Minutes of Evidence and Appendices.
ISBN 0 10 296788 1.   HMSO   1988 18.50

Radio: Choices and Opportunities. A Consultative
Document. Cm 92.
ISBN 0 10 100922 4.   HMSO   1987   5.00

Report of the Committee on Financing the BBC.
(Chairman: Professor Alan Peacock, DSC, FBA.)
Cmnd 9824.
ISBN 0 10 198240 2.   HMSO   1986 10.80

The ITC Programme Code.   ITC

The ITC Code of Advertising Standards
and Practice.   ITC

The ITC Code of Programme Sponsorship.   ITC

The Radio Authority Code of Advertising
Standards and Practice and
Programme Sponsorship.   Radio Authority

The Radio Authority Programme Code on
News Programmes and Coverage of Matters
of Political or Industrial Controversy or
Relating to Current Public Policy.   Radio Authority

*The Radio Authority Programme Code on Violence,
Sex, Taste and Decency, Children and Young
People, Appeals for Donations, Religion and
Other Matters.*   Radio Authority

£

Other Publications

The BBC: The First Fifty Years. Briggs, Asa.   Out of
ISBN 0 19 212971 6.   Oxford University Press   1985 print

Broadcasting Data Systems: Teletext and RDS.
Mothersole, P. L. and White, N.W.   Focal Press   1992 14.95
ISBN 0 240 513541.

*Broadcasting in the United Kingdom: A Guide to
Information Sources.* Macdonald, Barrie.
Second revised edition.
ISBN 0 7201 2086 1.   Mansell   1993 50.00

Broadcasting: the New Law.
Reville, N. ISBN 0 406 00137 5.   Butterworth   1991 16.00

*Cameras in the Commons: the study for the
Hansard Society on the Televising of the
House of Commons.* Hetherington A.
ISBN 0 900432 22 5.   Hansard Society   1990 10.00

Conversations with the World. Tusa, J.   BBC Books   1990   7.99
ISBN 0 563 360082.

The History of Broadcasting in the United Kingdom.

Vol 1. The Birth of Broadcasting.   Out of
ISBN 0 19 212926 0.   Oxford University Press   1961 print

£

Vol 2. The Golden Age of Wireless.   Out of
ISBN 0 19 212930 9.   Oxford University Press   1965   print

Vol 3. The War of Words.   Out of
ISBN 0 19 212956 2.   Oxford University Press   1970   print

Vol 4. Sound and Vision.   Out of
ISBN 0 19 212967 8.   Oxford University Press   1989   print

Independent Television in Britain. Sendall, Bernard.
Vol 1. Origin and Foundation, 1946–62.
ISBN 0 333 30941 3.   Macmillan   1982 38.00

Vol 2. Expansion and Change, 1958–68.
ISBN 0 333 30942 1.   Macmillan   1983 38.00

Vol 3.Politics and Control, 1968–80.
Potter, J. ISBN 0 333 33019 6.   Macmillan   1988 35.00

Vol 4. Companies and Programmes, 1968–80.
Potter, J. ISBN 0 333 455543 6.   Macmillan   1990 45.00

*The Invisible Medium: Public, Commercial and
Community Radio.* Lewis, P.M. and Booth, J.
ISBN 0 333 42366 6.   Macmillan   1989 11.99

*Let Truth Be Told: 50 Years of BBC External
Broadcasting.* Mansell, Gerard.
ISBN 0 297 78158 8.   Weidenfeld & Nicolson   1982 16.95

*The Media in Britain Today: The Facts,
the Figures.* Veljanovski, C.   News International   1990 25.00

£

A Social History of British Broadcasting,
Volume One 1922-1939: Serving the Nation.
Scannell, P. and Cardiff, D.
ISBN 0 631 17543 1.　　　　　　　Blackwell　1991　30.00

Teletalk: A Dictionary of Broadcasting
Terms. Jarvis, P. (editor).
ISBN 0 948694 40 8.　　BBC Television Training　1991　6.50

Television Licence Fee: A Study for the
Home Office. Management Summary.
PriceWaterhouse. ISBN 0 11 341003 4.　　HMSO　1990　3.20

Annual Publications
BBC Annual Report and Accounts.　　　　　BBC
Report of the Broadcasting Complaints
Commission.　　　　　　　　　　　　HMSO
Broadcasting Standards Council Annual Report.　BSC
Channel Four Television Report
and Accounts.　　　Channel Four Television
Film and Television Handbook.　British Film Institute
The Independent Television Commission
Annual Report and Accounts.　　　　　　ITC
Radio Authority Annual Report and Financial
Statements.　　　　　Radio Authority
S4C Report and Accounts.　　　　　　S4C

Index

Printed in the UK for HMSO.
Dd.296526, 8/93, C30, 51-2423, 5673.